Monkey Business

PROBOSCIS MONKEYS

Gillian Gosman

PowerKiDS
press™
New York

Published in 2012 by The Rosen Publishing Group, Inc.
29 East 21st Street, New York, NY 10010

First Edition

Editor: Jennifer Way
Book Design: Kate Laczynski

Photo Credits: Cover, pp. 1, 4, 8 iStockphoto/Thinkstock; p. 5 © www.iStockphoto.com/Andrew Fildes; pp. 6, 10, 12, 17 (left), 18 Shutterstock.com; pp. 7, 13 (left) Tim Laman/National Geographic/Getty Images; p. 9 Visuals Unlimited, Inc./Joe McDonald/Getty Images; p. 11 © www.iStockphoto.com/Kjersti Joergensen; p. 13 (right) Hemera/Thinkstock; pp. 14–15 © Peter Lilja/age fotostock; p. 16 Andrea Pistolesi/Getty Images; p. 17 (right) © Cyril Ruoso/Peter Arnold, Inc.; p. 19 © www.iStockphoto.com/miskani; p. 20 Anup Shah/Digital Vision/Thinkstock; p. 21 Jami Tarris/Getty Images; p. 22 Visuals Unlimited, Inc./Thomas Marent/Getty Images.

Library of Congress Cataloging-in-Publication Data

Gosman, Gillian.
  Proboscis monkeys / by Gillian Gosman. — 1st ed.
      p. cm. — (Monkey business)
  Includes index.
  ISBN 978-1-4488-5024-2 (library binding) — ISBN 978-1-4488-5183-6 (pbk.) — ISBN 978-1-4488-5184-3 (6-pack)
  1. Proboscis monkey—Juvenile literature. I. Title.
  QL737.P93G675 2012
  599.8—dc22
                                2011003074

Manufactured in the United States of America

CPSIA Compliance Information: Batch #WS11PK: For Further Information contact Rosen Publishing, New York, New York at 1-800-237-9932

Contents

MEET THE PROBOSCIS MONKEY

A **proboscis** is a long, bendable nose. An elephant's trunk is a proboscis. The proboscis monkey is named for its big, reddish pink nose. Scientists are not sure why it has this neat nose. Some believe its big nose helps this large **primate**

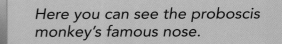

Here you can see the proboscis monkey's famous nose.

Like most other monkeys, the proboscis monkey is a skilled tree climber.

cool down. They also think the nose helps it communicate and show fellow proboscis monkeys how old or powerful it is.

The proboscis monkey is a **species** that lives in Southeast Asia. This book will introduce you to this unusual monkey and teach you more about its life and its behavior.

GET TO KNOW THIS NOSE!

Proboscis monkeys have reddish brown and gray fur. They have pink, hairless faces, which makes their big noses the center of attention. The proboscis can be up to 7 inches (18 cm) long. This big nose **amplifies**, or makes louder, the monkey's calls and honks. These noises are often used to tell other proboscis monkeys that danger is near.

Male proboscis monkeys, like the one shown here, have much larger proboscises than do females.

When the proboscis monkey gets scared, its proboscis fills with blood. This makes the nose swell. A swollen nose makes their honks even louder. Proboscis monkeys also honk to let members of their group feel close to one another.

Scientists think that female monkeys might find males with bigger noses more attractive because those males can make the loudest calls.

AN OLD WORLD MONKEY

Proboscis monkeys are known as **Old World** monkeys. These monkeys live in Africa, Asia, and the Middle East. Proboscis monkeys can be found only in Borneo. Borneo is a large island in the South China Sea, just north of Australia. There are high mountains, long rivers, deep caves, and large forests of every kind there.

Borneo, where proboscis monkeys live, is the third-largest island in the world. The island is part of the countries of Brunei, Malaysia, and Indonesia.

Old World monkeys have certain traits in common. As do other Old World monkeys, proboscis monkeys have tails. These tails help them stay balanced while climbing. They cannot grip things, though, as the tails of **New World** monkeys can. Proboscis monkeys and other Old World monkeys do have **opposable** thumbs for gripping things, though.

Proboscis monkeys walk mostly on all fours. Here you can see the monkey using its tail for balance, rather than to hold on to the tree branch.

LIFE IN BORNEO

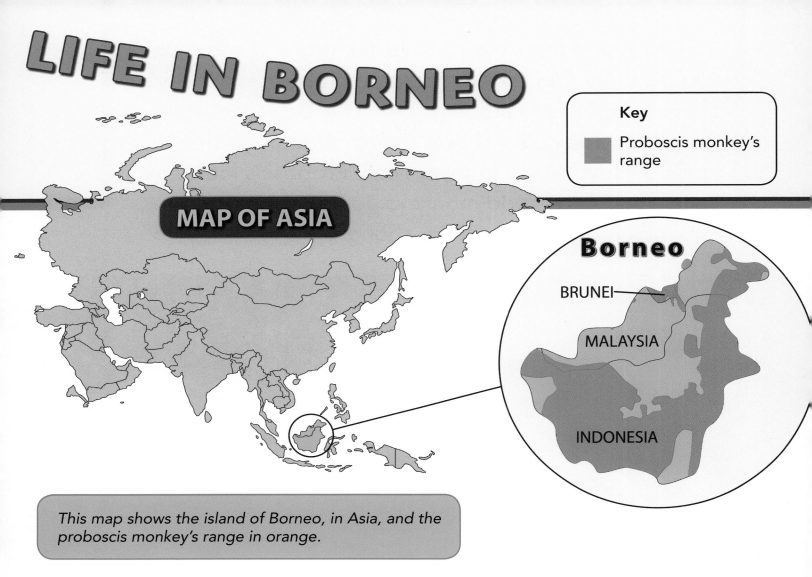

Key

Proboscis monkey's range

MAP OF ASIA

Borneo

BRUNEI

MALAYSIA

INDONESIA

This map shows the island of Borneo, in Asia, and the proboscis monkey's range in orange.

Proboscis monkeys usually live near water and wetlands in Borneo. They live among mangrove forests along rivers and **estuaries**. An estuary is where a river flows into the ocean. Proboscis monkeys also live in swamps and in hot, wet rain forests. They move from one area to the next in search of food.

The proboscis monkey's habitat is usually very warm. The temperature stays close to 80° F (27° C) year-round. It is also very wet. In one year, Borneo's wetlands might get 100 inches (254 cm) of rain.

These proboscis monkeys are in a mangrove tree. Proboscis monkeys stay close to the water most of the time. They are rarely more than .4 mile (600 m) from a river.

FUN FACT

Leafy mangrove trees put down their roots in the sandy bottoms of rivers and estuaries. Mangrove forests are home to many living things. Mangrove forests protect the shoreline from waves, weather, and pollution.

WHAT PROBOSCIS MONKEYS EAT

Proboscis monkeys look like they have swollen bellies. This is because their stomachs are very large and divided into different parts. Each part works to digest, or break down, different kinds of plants. Their stomachs and what is inside them make up about one-quarter of a proboscis monkey's weight!

Here you can see the proboscis monkey's big belly. Proboscis monkeys eat only unripe fruit. The sugars in ripe fruits can cause bloating that can be deadly to the monkey.

Thanks to these special stomachs, proboscis monkeys can eat many different plants. They can even eat plants that are poisonous, or deadly, to other animals. They eat leaves, seeds, flowers, unripe fruit, and shoots from mangrove trees. They also eat insects, caterpillars, and larvae.

Proboscis monkeys tend to eat twice each day, once in the morning and again in the early evening.

These are leaves and shoots on a mangrove tree.

PROBOSCIS HAREMS

Most proboscis monkeys live in harem groups. A harem group has one male, between two and seven females, and their offspring. The total number of harem members is usually between 3 and 32 monkeys. There are also all-male proboscis monkey groups.

Proboscis monkey harem groups do almost everything together. They sleep together in trees near the water. They go inland during the day to look for food together, they wander the forest

Here is a group of proboscis monkeys. Females usually stay in the group into which they were born. Males leave their birth group to join all-male groups at around 18 months of age. When they are a little older, they will find harems to take over.

together, and they watch for **predators** together. Groups of proboscis monkeys live peacefully alongside other proboscis monkey harems. The male monkeys almost never fight over land, food, or female monkeys.

FUN FACT

Leopards, large snakes, lizards, and other large animals hunt the proboscis monkey. The members of a group look out for one another!

MONKEYING AROUND

The proboscis monkey is mostly **arboreal**. This means that these monkeys spend a great deal of time in trees. They get around in trees by jumping or swinging from branch to branch, by climbing, and by walking along branches on all fours.

Even though proboscis monkeys are arboreal, they are never far from water. In fact, they are

This proboscis monkey is jumping from a tree to the water.

great swimmers. They swim mostly to cross rivers. The skin between this monkey's fingers and toes is webbed. This extra skin forms a wide pad that helps the monkeys swim. Sometimes a proboscis monkey will jump from the treetops into the water with a big belly flop!

Proboscis monkeys do not go into areas where there are no trees. They find it safer and easier to get around in forested areas.

FUN FACT

A proboscis monkey can hold its breath and swim underwater for up to 65 feet (20 m)!

Webbed fingers and toes make proboscis monkeys faster at swimming than they are at walking.

MALES AND FEMALES

Male proboscis monkeys are larger than females. A male might be nearly 30 inches (76 cm) tall and weigh nearly 50 pounds (23 kg). A female might be only 24 inches (61 cm) tall and weigh just 15 pounds (7 kg).

When females are five years old and males are seven years old, they are ready to **mate**, or have

This is an adult male proboscis monkey. Male and female proboscis monkeys look more different from each other than any other primate.

babies. A female might show a male that she is ready to mate by puckering her lips or shaking her head at him. Females and males often come together to mate between February and November. A baby grows inside its mother for about five and a half months before being born.

This is an adult female proboscis monkey. Arboreal monkeys like the proboscis monkey actually have their babies while sitting in trees!

A baby proboscis monkey weighs just 1 pound (454 g). Its face is dark blue. After two months, its face turns gray. By the time the baby is nine months old, its face is a pinkish cream. Even at birth, the monkey has a large, turned-up nose. The nose will continue to grow throughout its life.

Here is a female proboscis monkey and her baby, which still has a dark blue face.

The baby proboscis monkey stays close to its mother for the first year of its life. She carries her baby, gives it milk, and grooms its fur for the first seven months of its life. In the wild, a proboscis monkey might live to be 10 years old. In zoos, proboscis monkeys have lived to be 25 years old.

This young proboscis monkey is getting the hang of climbing trees!

AN ENDANGERED MONKEY

In Borneo, people have been cutting down trees for wood and to clear land for farms. This takes away the natural habitat of animals like the proboscis monkey. It means the monkeys have nowhere to live, find food, and raise their young.

Shown here is the Danum Valley Conservation Area, in the Malaysian part of Borneo. This is a national park where proboscis monkeys live. The land there is protected from being completely cleared.

Because of habitat loss, proboscis monkeys are considered an **endangered** species. There are laws that protect the proboscis monkey from being hunted. Many live in national parks where the lands are not allowed to be cleared. Hopefully these efforts will help the proboscis monkey's numbers grow and thrive in their natural habitat.

Glossary

amplifies (AM-pluh-fyz) Makes louder.

arboreal (ahr-BOR-ee-ul) Having to do with trees.

endangered (in-DAYN-jerd) In danger of no longer existing.

estuaries (ES-choo-wer-eez) Areas of water where the ocean tide meets a river.

mate (MAYT) To come together to make babies.

New World (NOO WURLD) North America and South America.

Old World (OHLD WURLD) The part of the world that includes Asia, Africa, and Europe.

opposable (uh-POH-zuh-bel) Able to hold digits on a hand or foot together.

predators (PREH-duh-terz) Animals that kill other animals for food.

primate (PRY-mayt) The group of animals that are more advanced than others and includes monkeys, gorillas, and people.

proboscis (pruh-BAH-sus) A long, flexible snout, such as an elephant's trunk or the proboscis monkey's nose.

species (SPEE-sheez) One kind of living thing. All people are one species.

Index

B
behavior, 5
blood, 7
Borneo, 8, 10, 22
branch(es), 16

D
danger, 6

E
estuaries, 10

F
face(s), 6, 20
female(s), 14, 18–19
food, 10, 14–15, 22
fruit, 13
fur, 6, 21

G
group(s), 7, 14–15

H
habitat loss, 22
honks, 6–7

I
island, 8

L
life, 5, 20–21

M
Middle East, 8

N
nose(s), 4–7, 20

P
predators, 15
primate, 4
proboscis, 4, 6–7

S
scientists, 4
South China Sea, 8
Southeast Asia, 5
species, 5, 22

T
tails, 9
thumbs, 9
trunk, 4

W
wetlands, 10–11

Web Sites

Due to the changing nature of Internet links, PowerKids Press has developed an online list of Web sites related to the subject of this book. This site is updated regularly. Please use this link to access the list:
www.powerkidslinks.com/monk/probosci/